MAYER SMITH

The Wealth Beneath Her Struggles

Copyright © 2025 by Mayer Smith

All rights reserved. No part of this publication may be reproduced, stored or transmitted in any form or by any means, electronic, mechanical, photocopying, recording, scanning, or otherwise without written permission from the publisher. It is illegal to copy this book, post it to a website, or distribute it by any other means without permission.

This novel is entirely a work of fiction. The names, characters and incidents portrayed in it are the work of the author's imagination. Any resemblance to actual persons, living or dead, events or localities is entirely coincidental.

Mayer Smith asserts the moral right to be identified as the author of this work.

Mayer Smith has no responsibility for the persistence or accuracy of URLs for external or third-party Internet Websites referred to in this publication and does not guarantee that any content on such Websites is, or will remain, accurate or appropriate.

Designations used by companies to distinguish their products are often claimed as trademarks. All brand names and product names used in this book and on its cover are trade names, service marks, trademarks and registered trademarks of their respective owners. The publishers and the book are not associated with any product or vendor mentioned in this book. None of the companies referenced within the book have endorsed the book.

First edition

*This book was professionally typeset on Reedsy.
Find out more at reedsy.com*

Contents

1	A Chance Encounter	1
2	The Connection	7
3	A Mysterious Gift	14
4	The Secret Meeting	20
5	A Sudden Disappearance	27
6	The Revelation	34
7	The Confrontation	41
8	The Past Unveiled	48
9	A Dangerous Rival	55
10	A Test of Trust	62
11	The Unraveling	69
12	The Breaking Point	76
13	A Risky Gamble	83
14	The Final Test	89
15	The Truth	96

One

A Chance Encounter

The wind rustled the leaves of the trees as Zara trudged down the narrow street, the weight of her responsibilities bearing down on her. She wasn't a stranger to hard work, but lately, it felt like she had been drowning in an unrelenting tide of problems. The bills, the long hours at her underpaid job, and the feeling that her life was stuck in a never-ending loop of disappointments. Zara had dreamed of more—of a life full of purpose, adventure, and maybe even a little bit of love. But lately, all those dreams seemed to be fading, slipping further away with each passing day.

It was a gray, overcast afternoon when Zara found herself on the familiar path to her favorite café, a small hole-in-the-wall that offered the kind of comforting solitude she needed. The smell of freshly brewed coffee was like a balm to her soul as she entered the warm space, the soft murmur of conversation and the clink of cups filling the air. Zara made her way to the counter, greeted by the barista who knew her well by now. She ordered her usual—a strong black coffee—and took a seat at the back of the café, near the window.

She looked out at the rain that had started to fall, the droplets streaking down the glass like the tears she had longed to shed but never allowed herself to. The view was familiar, comforting, but it didn't offer the escape she needed. She pulled out her phone, scrolling aimlessly through her social media feed, her eyes catching on posts of vacations, engagements, and promotions—things that felt so far out of her reach. The feeling of being stuck deepened, and she let out a sigh, sinking deeper into her chair.

That was when she saw him.

He was sitting at the table near the door, his back to the window. His appearance was unremarkable at first glance—a man in his mid-thirties with messy, unkempt hair and a worn-out jacket that seemed out of place in the cozy café. His clothes were frayed at the edges, the kind of attire you'd expect from someone who didn't have much to their name. He wasn't particularly tall, but there was something about his posture, the way he sat hunched over the table, as though carrying the weight of the world on his shoulders.

Zara had always been observant, perhaps too much so. She found herself studying him, her curiosity piqued by the quiet intensity he exuded. There was something captivating about him—something in the way he seemed so lost in thought, as though the world around him didn't matter. It was as though he was someone who had learned how to shut everything out, to retreat into his own thoughts.

As she watched him, he looked up for a moment, and their eyes met. For a brief second, time seemed to freeze. His eyes were deep and dark, like pools of mystery that Zara found herself drawn to. There was a flicker of recognition in his gaze, something almost familiar, though they had never met. It was as though he had seen through her, understood the weight she carried, even without her saying a word. Zara quickly looked away, embarrassed by the intensity of the moment. But as she turned her head, she couldn't shake the feeling that there was more to him than met the eye.

A few minutes passed, and Zara's curiosity began to get the best of her. She stole a glance in his direction again, only to find him staring at his coffee cup, his fingers tracing the rim absentmindedly. His expression was blank, yet there was an undercurrent of sadness that seemed to cling to him. Zara couldn't help but wonder what had brought him to this café, why he seemed so lost.

Her thoughts were interrupted by the barista placing her coffee in front of her. She thanked him, taking the steaming cup in her hands and savoring the warmth as it spread through her fingers. She took a sip, letting the bitterness of the coffee ground her, but her mind kept drifting back to the man at the other table.

What was his story?

Without fully thinking it through, Zara stood up and walked over to his table. She hesitated for a moment, unsure of what to say, but something inside of her—some deep, unexplained pull—urged her to act. She cleared her throat before speaking.

"Excuse me," she said softly, her voice a little unsure, "I couldn't help but notice you're here alone. I come here often, too. Do you mind if I join you?"

The man looked up slowly, his dark eyes studying her for a moment before he nodded, a small, barely noticeable smile curling at the corner of his lips.

"Sure," he replied, his voice low and gravelly, as though he hadn't spoken in a while. "Please, sit."

Zara hesitated for only a second before sliding into the chair across from him. She wasn't sure why she felt compelled to do this, to reach out to someone she didn't even know. But something about his presence made her feel... safe, in a way she hadn't felt in a long time.

"I'm Zara," she said, offering her hand. He shook it, his grip firm but gentle.

"Alex," he replied simply, his eyes still locked on hers.

There was a long pause, the weight of the silence pressing between them. Zara didn't know what to say next, but she felt the need to break the tension.

"So," she began, her voice lighter, "what brings you here today?"

Alex took a deep breath, his eyes shifting toward the window, as though he were contemplating the right words. "Just… thinking," he said, his voice distant. "I like this place. It's quiet. Gives me time to think."

Zara nodded, understanding the need for solitude. She didn't press further, allowing him to speak when he was ready.

"You're not from around here, are you?" she asked, trying to make conversation, though she couldn't quite shake the feeling that there was more to him than he was letting on.

"No," he replied, his gaze briefly flicking to her before returning to his coffee. "Just passing through."

"Passing through?" Zara echoed, intrigued. "That sounds… mysterious."

Alex's lips twitched upward, but it wasn't a full smile. "I guess it is, in a way."

Zara was quiet for a moment, taking a sip of her coffee as she tried to make sense of the man sitting across from her. There was something in his eyes that spoke of deep pain, of someone who had seen far too much in life. His disheveled appearance was at odds with the depth of emotion he carried. She couldn't help but wonder what had brought him to this point.

"So, what do you do?" she asked, unable to resist the question.

"You seem… different."

Alex's expression softened slightly, and for a moment, he didn't answer. It was as though the question had caught him off guard.

"I'm… between things," he said after a long pause, his voice trailing off.

Zara sensed there was more he wasn't saying, but she didn't push. Instead, she smiled, deciding not to press any further. There was something endearing about his reluctance to talk, something that made her want to know him more, to unravel the layers he had built around himself.

"Well, I'll let you get back to your thinking," Zara said, rising from her seat. "But I'm glad we talked. Maybe I'll see you again sometime."

Alex gave a small nod, his gaze lingering on her for a moment longer than she expected. "Maybe."

As Zara walked away, her heart raced with a mix of emotions—curiosity, intrigue, and an undeniable pull that she couldn't explain. There was something about Alex that left her wanting more. Something mysterious, something hidden beneath the surface. And for the first time in a long while, Zara felt a spark of hope, as though she might have just met someone who could change everything.

But what was Alex truly hiding?

Two

The Connection

The days that followed Zara's brief encounter with Alex at the café were filled with an odd sense of anticipation. She couldn't shake the memory of their conversation—his quiet, thoughtful manner, the depth in his eyes that seemed to speak volumes. She hadn't expected it to be anything more than a fleeting moment, an odd exchange with a stranger that she'd forget about in the rush of her everyday life. But the pull of his presence lingered, a quiet tug at the back of her mind, demanding her attention.

It wasn't long before she found herself walking past the café again, almost without thinking. The weather had shifted; the skies were brighter now, the air warmer, as though the world had decided to follow suit and bring a touch of hope into her life. The café, her usual sanctuary, was bustling with the sounds of conversation and clinking cups as people went about their day.

Zara hesitated outside, her hand resting on the door for a moment. She wasn't sure why she had come back, why she was suddenly so eager to see him again. Perhaps it was the curiosity that still gnawed at her, or the subtle sense of connection she had felt with Alex—a connection that didn't quite make sense but felt undeniable nonetheless.

Taking a deep breath, Zara pushed open the door and stepped inside, scanning the room. There, sitting at the same corner table near the window, was Alex. He hadn't noticed her yet, his focus entirely on the open book in front of him, the pages slowly turning as he read. He looked just as she remembered—disheveled, quiet, lost in his own world—but there was something different this time. The weight of the world seemed to press more heavily on him, as though the shadows beneath his eyes had deepened overnight.

Zara's heart gave a quick, unexpected flutter as she walked toward his table. She didn't even pause to think; her legs seemed to carry her there on their own, driven by some magnetic force she didn't fully understand. When she reached his table, she cleared her throat softly.

"Mind if I join you again?" she asked, her voice slightly more confident than the last time they spoke.

Alex looked up from his book, his expression unreadable at first. His dark eyes locked onto hers, and for a brief moment, Zara felt that familiar sense of being seen. He wasn't just looking at her; he was looking through her, as though he knew exactly what she was thinking before she even said a word.

"Of course," he said, his voice low and warm. "Sit. It's good to see you again."

Zara smiled, slightly taken aback by the warmth in his voice. She took the seat across from him, once again feeling a strange sense of comfort settle over her, as if she had found a place where she truly belonged.

"I didn't expect to find you here," she admitted, stirring her coffee absentmindedly. "It seems like we keep crossing paths."

Alex smiled, though it was brief, a flicker of amusement in his eyes. "I suppose it's fate," he said lightly, though his tone suggested there was more to it than just coincidence.

There was a moment of silence as Zara waited for him to elaborate, but Alex simply returned his attention to his book. Zara tried to ignore the gnawing feeling in her chest, the way her curiosity about him was growing stronger by the minute. She couldn't quite explain it, but something about Alex made her want to know everything—his past, his present, his dreams, his fears. There was a mystery to him that she couldn't ignore.

"So, what's the book?" she asked, trying to steer the conversation toward something more neutral.

Alex glanced down at the book in his hands, then back at her. "Oh, it's just something I've been reading to pass the time.

Philosophy, mostly."

Zara nodded, intrigued. "Philosophy, huh? That's... unexpected."

He shrugged slightly, a faint smile tugging at the corners of his lips. "I suppose I've always found it easier to understand the world through abstract ideas than through the mess of everyday life."

Zara considered this, her fingers absently tapping the edge of her cup. There was something about Alex's way of thinking, his introspective nature, that resonated with her. She, too, often found herself lost in her thoughts, contemplating the deeper questions of life. She wondered if that was part of the connection she had felt the first time they met—the sense that they both saw the world through a lens of complexity, yet were constantly seeking simplicity.

"You don't seem like the average person who'd read philosophy," Zara said, her eyes narrowing playfully. "I mean, not that I'm judging, but you don't exactly come across as someone who spends their time pondering the meaning of existence."

Alex's lips quirked into a half-smile, but there was a flicker of something more in his eyes, something deeper. "Appearances can be deceiving," he replied quietly.

Zara felt a sharp sting of realization at his words. She had assumed so much about him based on his clothes, his demeanor—the way he had appeared when she first met him. But now, sitting across from him, she couldn't help but feel like there was so much more beneath the surface that she hadn't even begun to understand.

"Tell me about yourself," Zara said before she could stop herself. "I feel like there's so much about you that I don't know."

Alex paused for a long moment, his fingers stilling on the pages of his book as his gaze shifted to the side. His silence was not uncomfortable, but it made Zara wonder what was going on inside his mind. Finally, he set the book down on the table, his eyes meeting hers once again.

"I don't know what there is to tell," he said, his voice soft, almost reluctant. "I'm just… a man trying to figure things out. That's all."

Zara's curiosity was piqued even more. His words were vague, but the way he said them suggested a life full of complexity and unanswered questions. She could sense that he was hiding something—something that weighed heavily on him, something he wasn't ready to share.

"So, what's your story?" she asked, leaning forward slightly, her tone more earnest. "You've got to have a story. Everyone does."

For the first time, Alex's eyes darkened slightly, his expression shifting to one of guardedness. It was subtle, but Zara caught it. He wasn't used to being asked these kinds of questions, or at least not by someone like her.

"I guess I'm not really the kind of person who shares their story," Alex said, his voice taking on a distant tone. "Some things are better left unsaid."

Zara's heart skipped a beat at his words, a chill running down her spine. She wasn't sure why, but she sensed that he wasn't just talking about small, insignificant details. There was something much bigger, much more important, that he was holding back. Something that would change everything if she knew the truth.

For a long moment, neither of them spoke. The silence between them hung heavy, charged with unspoken words, with the weight of emotions neither of them was quite ready to express. Zara wanted to press further, to push him to open up, but she sensed that now was not the time. She couldn't force him to tell her everything, no matter how much she wanted to understand him.

Instead, she leaned back in her chair, taking a deep breath. "Okay," she said quietly, "I won't push. But... just know, I'm here if you ever want to talk."

Alex met her gaze, his eyes softening slightly, as though he were contemplating her words. A small smile tugged at the corner of his lips, though it was tinged with something more—a quiet acknowledgment, perhaps, of the connection that had begun to form between them.

"Thank you," he said, his voice low. "I might take you up on that... someday."

The Connection

Zara smiled, though she couldn't shake the feeling that she had just scraped the surface of something much deeper. As she sat there, across from Alex, she realized that the connection they shared wasn't just about the conversations they had. It was about something unspoken, something that drew them together despite the walls they both had built around themselves.

And as the minutes ticked by, Zara couldn't help but wonder—what was Alex hiding? What was it that he wasn't telling her? And why did it feel like the answers to those questions might change everything between them?

For the first time in a long while, Zara felt the pull of something more—a mystery she couldn't resist, a man she couldn't quite figure out. And she couldn't shake the feeling that, whether she was ready for it or not, her life was about to change in ways she couldn't even begin to understand.

Three

A Mysterious Gift

Zara had never been one for surprises. She had always preferred the predictability of her routine, the comfort of knowing what each day would bring. But there was something about the way Alex had slipped into her life that made her feel as though she were walking a thin line between her ordinary world and a reality that was far more unpredictable—far more dangerous. Each time they met, the tension between them grew, not in the way that one might expect from a romance but in something deeper, more unsettling.

It had been a week since their last conversation, and while Zara had told herself that she wouldn't obsess over the mysterious man who had come into her life, she found herself thinking about him more often than she cared to admit. It wasn't just his presence, though that alone was enough to make her stomach flutter. It was the way he carried himself, the quiet intensity in his eyes, the layers of emotion that seemed to radiate just beneath the surface. Zara felt like she was only scratching the surface of who he really was, and for some reason, that nagging feeling of curiosity had become unbearable.

She had gone back to the café the next day, hoping to see him again, but he hadn't been there. Days passed, and the memory of their last conversation began to fade, replaced by the overwhelming demands of her life. Work was as difficult as ever, the bills piled higher with each passing day, and her sense of hopelessness returned. She needed an escape. She needed something to lift her spirits, to remind her that there was more to life than the mundane cycle she had fallen into.

It was late afternoon when she received a text message that sent a shiver down her spine.

I've left something for you. Please meet me at the café.

The message was from Alex. Zara's heart raced as she read the words, her fingers trembling slightly as she typed out a response.

What's going on, Alex? What is this about?

There was no immediate reply, and for a moment, Zara considered ignoring it. Maybe it was a mistake—maybe she was reading too much into it. But her curiosity won out, and before she could stop herself, she grabbed her jacket and headed out the door.

The Wealth Beneath Her Struggles

The café was quieter than usual when Zara arrived. It was still early enough in the evening that the usual crowd hadn't settled in, and the soft hum of conversation was punctuated by the clinking of cups and the hiss of steam from the espresso machine. She scanned the room, half-expecting to see Alex sitting at their usual table, but there was no sign of him.

Zara felt a twinge of disappointment. She had come all this way, hoping for something—anything—that would explain the strange message. But there was nothing.

She turned to leave, but something caught her eye. On a small table near the back, next to the window, was a neatly wrapped box. It was small, the kind of gift one might give for an anniversary or a special occasion, but there was no tag, no note. Only the box itself, sitting there as if waiting for her.

A strange unease settled over Zara as she approached the table. She could feel her pulse quicken, her breath shallow. It was as though the room had grown colder, the air thick with tension. The box sat there, taunting her, its sleek exterior gleaming in the soft light of the café. Without thinking, Zara reached for it, her fingers brushing the delicate paper. The ribbon was neatly tied, and the box was surprisingly heavy for its size.

She hesitated for a moment, her mind racing with questions. What was this? What did it mean? And why had Alex left it for her?

Unable to resist, she untied the ribbon and peeled back the paper, revealing a small wooden box beneath. It was carved

A Mysterious Gift

with intricate patterns, the wood polished to a smooth sheen. There was no indication of who it had come from, but Zara knew, deep down, that this was Alex's doing. She could feel his presence in the very act of opening it.

Her hands trembled as she lifted the lid of the box. Inside was something unexpected—a delicate silver bracelet, encrusted with tiny diamonds that glittered in the light. The bracelet was simple but elegant, the kind of thing one might wear to a gala or a formal event. It was beautiful, no doubt, but it also felt out of place in the dimly lit café, in this world of everyday struggles that Zara found herself trapped in.

As she lifted the bracelet from the box, she noticed something else beneath it—a small folded piece of paper. Zara's heart skipped a beat as she unfolded it carefully, her fingers trembling as she read the words scrawled on the page in a neat, elegant handwriting.

For the woman who sees beyond appearances. Wear this, and remember that there is more to you than what the world shows. I hope this gift reminds you of that.

Zara's breath caught in her throat. The words seemed to echo in her mind, reverberating through her thoughts. What did he mean by that? What was he trying to tell her? And why had he chosen this moment, this gift, to make such a cryptic declaration?

She glanced around the café, half-expecting to see Alex standing in the corner, watching her, but there was no sign of him. The room was empty, save for a few patrons in the back. She was alone, with only the bracelet and the note to keep her company.

The bracelet felt impossibly heavy in her hand, its weight a stark reminder of the mystery that was unfolding before her. Alex had given her this gift for a reason, but what was that reason? Was it an attempt to get closer to her, to pull her into his world of secrets and shadows? Or was it something more—something deeper, something that could change everything between them?

Zara slipped the bracelet onto her wrist, its cool surface pressing against her skin. It fit perfectly, as though it had been made just for her. She couldn't help but feel a strange sense of connection to it, to Alex, even though she didn't understand any of it. It was as if the bracelet had somehow become a symbol of the invisible bond that had begun to form between them—a bond that was as mysterious and elusive as Alex himself.

But with the bracelet came the question that Zara couldn't shake: What did Alex want from her? What was he expecting? She had asked him so many questions before, but each time, he had deflected, avoiding the answers she so desperately sought. Now, with this gift, she couldn't help but feel as though she were being drawn into something far beyond her control.

As she sat there, the weight of the bracelet on her wrist, she felt the familiar stirrings of unease. The café, once a place of comfort, now felt suffocating. The walls seemed to close in around her, and she couldn't shake the feeling that something was about to happen—something that would change everything.

A Mysterious Gift

Zara stood up abruptly, her mind racing. She needed answers. She couldn't keep playing this game of cryptic messages and mysterious gifts. She needed to confront Alex. She needed to know what was really going on.

But as she walked toward the door, she paused. There, in the corner of the café, standing by the window, was Alex.

He was watching her, his dark eyes meeting hers with an intensity that made her heart race. His expression was unreadable, but there was something in the way he stood—something in the way his gaze locked onto hers—that sent a shiver down her spine.

Zara took a step toward him, her breath caught in her throat. The bracelet on her wrist felt heavier than ever. The mystery, the tension, it all came to a head in that moment.

Alex's lips curled into a faint, almost imperceptible smile. And in that moment, Zara realized that this wasn't just a simple gift. It was a message. And the questions she had been avoiding—questions about Alex, about the life he led, about the world he was hiding—were about to be answered.

But at what cost?

Four

The Secret Meeting

Zara couldn't shake the feeling that something had shifted, that the world around her had subtly but irrevocably changed. Since receiving the mysterious gift from Alex—a gift that had seemed both meaningful and unsettling—her thoughts had become consumed with him. She had spent days trying to piece together the meaning behind the bracelet, trying to decipher the cryptic note he had left for her. It wasn't just the gift itself that lingered in her mind, though. It was the strange, unsettling sense that Alex was hiding something—something deep and significant—and that she was being drawn deeper into a story she wasn't fully prepared for.

Her restless nights had turned into even more restless days. The café was no longer just a place where she went for coffee; it had become a site of tension, a place where fate seemed to constantly tug at her with its invisible strings. Alex had always been elusive, but now, he was even more so. He had stopped showing up at their usual meeting spot, and though Zara had searched for him several times, he had remained a ghost—always there, but never within reach.

That is, until tonight.

Zara hadn't expected the message when it came. She had been sitting in her apartment, nursing a half-drunk glass of wine, her mind too tired to focus on anything in particular, when her phone buzzed on the coffee table. At first, she had been too distracted to check it, but the persistent vibration made her glance at the screen.

I need to see you. Tonight. Meet me at 9 p.m. at the old warehouse on Elm Street.

Her heart stuttered in her chest as she read the message again, certain she had misunderstood. Elm Street was a run-down part of town, the kind of place where people went to disappear. A warehouse? Alex had always been quiet and mysterious, but this felt different—more dangerous. Her instinct screamed at her to ignore it, to walk away, but something else, something more compelling, urged her to go. After all, how could she resist? She was already too far gone, too tangled up in whatever Alex was hiding.

Her mind raced as she pulled on a coat and grabbed her bag, the streets outside her apartment darker than usual, the shadows seeming to stretch longer as she walked. She wasn't entirely sure what she was walking toward, but with each step, her pulse quickened. The thought of the warehouse—of that place on Elm Street—set her nerves alight. The air felt charged, as if the very ground she walked on was electric with anticipation.

When she arrived at Elm Street, the street was eerily quiet. The buildings loomed over her, their windows dark and lifeless. The warehouse was at the end of the block, a hulking structure of concrete and rusted metal. Its broken windows reflected the moonlight, casting long shadows that made the place look even more foreboding.

Zara hesitated at the entrance, her hand trembling as she reached for the door handle. Her breath came in shallow gasps, her heart pounding in her chest. What was Alex trying to tell her? Why had he asked her to meet him here, of all places? She could feel the weight of the night pressing down on her, making the atmosphere seem thicker, heavier. Every noise seemed amplified, the faint rustling of leaves in the wind, the far-off hum of distant traffic. She couldn't shake the feeling that she was being watched, that someone, or something, was lurking just out of sight.

The door creaked open, and Zara stepped inside.

The warehouse was dark, the only light coming from a single, flickering bulb that hung overhead. The air smelled of dust and old wood, and the sound of her footsteps echoed loudly in the empty space. Her eyes darted around, but she saw no one. The building seemed abandoned, save for the faint outline of crates and barrels in the distance.

She called out quietly, her voice barely a whisper. "Alex? Are you here?"

There was no answer, only the sound of her own voice bouncing off the cold walls. A chill ran down her spine, and she took a cautious step forward, her senses on high alert. What had she gotten herself into?

Just as she was about to turn and leave, a figure emerged from the shadows. It was Alex.

He looked different, more intense than the last time they had met. His usual casual demeanor was gone, replaced by a tension in his posture that made him seem almost unrecognizable. He was dressed in dark clothes, a long coat draped over his shoulders, his face partially obscured by the hood of his jacket. His eyes, however, were unmistakable. They were still the same dark, haunting eyes that had drawn her in from the very beginning.

Zara froze, her heart leaping into her throat. She hadn't expected to see him here, not like this. Not in this place. Not under these circumstances.

"Alex," she said, her voice barely audible, "What's going on? Why here?"

Alex stepped closer, his movements fluid but cautious. "You came," he said simply, as though her presence was the only thing that mattered. "I knew you would."

The Wealth Beneath Her Struggles

Zara swallowed hard, trying to steady her nerves. "Why this place? What do you want from me?"

Alex's gaze softened, but there was an edge to it that she couldn't quite place. "It's not about what I want," he replied quietly. "It's about what you need to understand."

Zara felt a chill run through her. "Understand? Understand what?"

Before he could answer, a loud clatter echoed through the warehouse, startling them both. Zara spun around, her breath caught in her throat, as shadows shifted near the back of the building. Someone else was here—someone who wasn't Alex.

Alex's face hardened, and without warning, he grabbed Zara's arm, pulling her toward a narrow stairwell in the corner of the room. "We need to go," he said urgently. "Now."

Her pulse raced as she stumbled to keep up with him. She had so many questions, so many things she didn't understand, but now wasn't the time to ask. She could hear footsteps behind them, the sound of someone—or something—getting closer. As they ascended the stairs, Alex's grip on her arm tightened, and Zara could feel the panic rising in her chest.

"Who's after us?" she asked, her voice trembling.

"Just trust me," Alex muttered, pushing open a door at the top of the stairs. "They're looking for me. But they don't know you're involved."

Zara's heart sank. "Involved? I don't even know what's going on!"

Alex didn't answer. Instead, he shoved open a door and pulled her into a small, dimly lit room. It smelled of old leather and dust, and there were papers scattered across the floor, along with strange symbols and maps that Zara didn't understand. She tried to catch her breath, her chest heaving as she looked at Alex, waiting for him to explain.

But instead, he took a step back, his eyes hardening. "You shouldn't have come here, Zara," he said, his voice low, almost cold. "But now that you're here, there's no turning back."

"What do you mean?" Zara whispered, her mind racing. "What is this? What is all of this?"

Alex reached into his coat pocket and pulled out a small envelope, handing it to her. "You're involved now, Zara," he said again, his tone more urgent this time. "This is bigger than anything you can imagine. But I didn't want to do this. I didn't want you to get caught up in it."

Zara took the envelope from him, her fingers brushing against his for the briefest moment. Her heart raced as she tore it open, revealing a stack of photographs inside. She spread them out on the floor in front of her, each image showing different locations—buildings, people, places Zara didn't recognize. But there was one thing that was the same in every photo: Alex.

In each one, he was standing in the background, his face

partially obscured, but always there. Always watching.

Zara's mind raced as she looked up at him. "What is this? Why are you in these photos?"

Alex's face twisted with frustration, his eyes darkening with something that looked like regret. "It's not what you think," he said, his voice harsh. "I'm not who you think I am. And now, you're part of this mess. They'll come for you now, too."

Zara stepped back, her heart pounding in her chest. "Who are you? What is all of this?"

Alex ran a hand through his hair, exhaling sharply. "I wanted to keep you safe, Zara. I tried. But you're already too close. The truth is coming, and you won't be able to escape it."

The room felt smaller suddenly, the walls closing in. Zara's mind whirled with questions she didn't even know how to ask. She had come to the warehouse expecting answers, but all she had found were more questions, more confusion.

And now, it seemed, there was no way out.

Five

A Sudden Disappearance

Zara's heart thudded in her chest, the adrenaline still coursing through her veins as she stared at the photographs scattered across the floor. Alex's face—no matter how hidden or shadowed—was always present. Each image was a silent accusation, a stark reminder that everything she had known about him, everything she thought she understood, had been a lie.

Her fingers trembled as she pulled the final photograph from the envelope, the last piece of the puzzle. This one was different, though. In this one, Alex wasn't just a distant figure. He was standing next to a man, his hand firmly on the shoulder of someone Zara didn't recognize. The man looked important—his clothes expensive, his posture commanding—but it was the way Alex stood beside him that caught Zara's attention. There was a familiarity in their poses, an ease in their relationship that made her stomach churn.

Suddenly, the air in the room felt too thick, too oppressive. Zara stood up abruptly, the floor creaking beneath her feet. Her pulse was pounding in her ears, and a cold sweat beaded on the back of her neck. She had come to this place seeking answers, but all she had found was confusion and more questions than ever before.

Alex stood silently across the room, watching her every move with a guarded expression. His lips were pressed into a tight line, his hands clenched at his sides. He wasn't the man she had met at the café—the man who had offered her quiet conversation and a sense of understanding. No, this Alex was someone else entirely. Someone dangerous. Someone who had clearly been hiding too much from her.

"What are you mixed up in?" Zara's voice was shaky, but she forced the words out, her chest tight with anxiety. "Who are these people? Why are you in these pictures?"

Alex took a step forward, his eyes never leaving hers. He opened his mouth as though to speak, but then the door behind them creaked. A loud bang echoed through the warehouse, followed by footsteps that grew louder by the second.

Zara's eyes widened in panic. "Alex, what's happening?" she demanded, her voice rising in alarm.

Alex didn't answer immediately. His eyes flickered toward the door, then back at her. Without warning, he moved quickly toward her, gripping her arm firmly, his fingers digging into her skin. Zara gasped as he pulled her toward the back of the room, urging her to move faster.

"Stay quiet," he hissed under his breath, his voice strained. "We have to go, now."

Zara barely had time to react before Alex shoved her through a narrow hallway that led deeper into the warehouse. Her thoughts were a blur, her breath coming in short, sharp gasps. What was going on? Who was coming? And why was Alex so determined to keep her out of sight? The sound of footsteps outside the door was growing louder, now accompanied by muffled voices. They were getting closer.

"I don't understand," Zara whispered, the panic rising in her chest as Alex pulled her through the maze of corridors. "Why didn't you tell me? Why didn't you explain?"

Alex's jaw clenched, but he didn't answer her. He was moving so quickly now that Zara had to half-jog to keep up, the cold air of the warehouse pressing in around them. Her heart was racing, her thoughts spinning wildly. What had she gotten herself into? What was the truth behind all the secrecy? She wanted to ask more questions, but she couldn't seem to get a word out.

They turned a corner, and Alex stopped abruptly, pulling her behind a stack of old crates. The footsteps outside had stopped, and Zara held her breath, trying to quiet her racing heartbeat. Alex's hand was still on her arm, but he wasn't looking at her. His gaze was fixed on something ahead of them—a small door that led out into the night.

The silence stretched on, unbearable and suffocating, as Zara's mind raced with possibilities. Had someone found them? Was she in danger? And if so, why?

Finally, Alex broke the silence. "They're here," he said, his voice low and tense. "They're looking for me. And now they know about you too."

Zara felt a cold wave of fear crash over her. "Who are they? What do they want?"

"I'll explain everything later," Alex replied, his voice hard, almost cold. "Just trust me. We don't have time."

Before Zara could respond, the sound of doors creaking open echoed through the warehouse. The men had arrived.

She felt a sudden surge of fear. Who were these men? They weren't just some casual visitors to the warehouse—they were methodical, purposeful. Their voices now carried over the space, low and hushed, but she could sense the danger in their presence.

"Where is he?" one of the voices asked, sharp and commanding. "He can't have gone far. Find him!"

Zara's breath caught in her throat. They were looking for Alex.

Her thoughts raced, panic threatening to take over. "Alex," she

A Sudden Disappearance

whispered urgently, her voice trembling. "What's going on? Why do they want you? Who are these people?"

Alex didn't answer at first. He was staring at the door ahead of them, his brow furrowed in concentration. "Stay here," he said quickly, almost too quickly. "I need to get out of here. I'll find a way to get you out."

Zara's heart leapt into her throat. "What do you mean, 'get me out'?" she demanded, her voice rising despite her fear. "Alex, you can't just leave me here!"

Alex looked at her then, his gaze intense. "You don't understand. I can't risk them finding you. You're safer here, out of sight. I'll come back for you. I swear I will."

Before Zara could protest, Alex turned and disappeared down the narrow hallway, moving swiftly, his footsteps barely audible. Zara's mind was spinning, her pulse hammering in her ears. She couldn't believe this was happening. The man she thought she knew, the man she thought she could trust, was slipping away from her—leaving her in a warehouse full of strangers and danger.

Zara stood frozen behind the crates, trying to steady her breathing, her mind working furiously. She couldn't just wait. She couldn't stay hidden while Alex risked everything to protect her.

She needed answers. She needed to know why Alex had kept so many secrets from her. Why had he dragged her into this world, and what exactly had he gotten himself involved in?

The sound of footsteps drew closer again, and this time, Zara could hear the distinct sound of two men talking, their voices growing louder as they approached.

"I told you he was here," one voice said. "He wouldn't be stupid enough to run."

The second voice grunted. "We'll see about that. Spread out. He can't have gone far."

Zara's heart pounded in her chest as she tried to steady her breathing, trying to remain as still and quiet as possible. Every nerve in her body screamed for her to move, to do something, anything, but fear rooted her to the spot. She wasn't alone anymore. The threat was closing in.

Minutes passed—long, agonizing minutes—and the footsteps seemed to grow louder, then softer, until Zara couldn't hear them anymore. Had they passed by? Or were they getting closer? She had no way of knowing. All she knew was that she had to make a decision.

She could stay here, hiding behind the crates, or she could follow Alex's advice and try to escape the building herself. But what if Alex was right? What if staying out of sight really was the only way to stay safe?

A sudden noise, sharp and unmistakable, echoed from the hallway. The unmistakable sound of a door slamming open.

A Sudden Disappearance

Zara's heart stopped.

Alex. Where was he?

Her body tensed, her mind racing. She couldn't sit still any longer. She had to act. But before she could make any move, a cold voice rang through the dark, "She's gone."

Her blood ran cold.

In that moment, Zara knew. The warehouse had swallowed her whole. And the man who had promised her answers... was gone.

Six

The Revelation

Zara sat frozen, her back pressed against the cold concrete wall of the warehouse, her breath shallow, her heart racing. The darkness around her felt suffocating, the silence that followed the sudden slam of the door only amplifying her fear. She had no idea what had just happened, why Alex had left so abruptly, or why the men who were searching for him seemed so determined to find him—find them.

Her thoughts were swirling in a chaotic frenzy. Why didn't he tell me? she wondered. Why had Alex kept everything so hidden? She had always sensed there was more to him, but now, with his disappearance and the men searching for him, she felt completely in the dark. Zara was alone, trapped in this warehouse, with no idea what to do or where to go.

The Revelation

The footsteps had faded, but the unease had settled deep into her bones. She glanced around the room, her gaze landing on the envelope and the photographs strewn across the floor. She reached down and picked them up, clutching the pieces of paper tightly in her trembling hands. They felt like the only tangible thing left, the only clues to understanding the mystery that Alex had drawn her into.

She needed to make sense of it all. She needed to understand what Alex was involved in, and why it seemed to have such dangerous consequences for her.

The door creaked open again, and Zara tensed, her muscles locked in a defensive stance. But this time, it wasn't one of the men searching for Alex. It was a familiar face—one she hadn't expected to see again.

"Zara," Alex's voice was low, barely above a whisper, as he stepped into the dim light of the room. His face was shadowed, his expression unreadable, but his eyes—his eyes were filled with something that unsettled her, something raw and unguarded.

"Alex," Zara breathed, relief flooding through her in waves, only to be quickly replaced by frustration. "Where did you go? Why did you leave me here? What's going on? Who are those people? What do they want from you?"

Alex didn't answer immediately. He stepped further into the room, closing the door behind him with a soft click. His eyes locked onto hers, and for a moment, there was silence—heavy, suffocating silence. He looked as if he were weighing something in his mind, deciding how much to reveal, how much to share.

"I know I owe you an explanation," he said quietly, his voice hoarse, as if the weight of his secrets had finally caught up with him. "But I never meant for any of this to happen. I didn't want you to get involved. This—" He waved a hand around the room, gesturing to the crates, the shadows, the very air around them that felt thick with secrets. "This isn't a world you should be a part of."

Zara's anger flared, mixing with the fear that had been steadily building inside her since he had disappeared. "You dragged me into this world, Alex!" she shot back, her voice trembling with emotion. "You showed up in my life, and you gave me all these pieces—these clues—and then you just disappear without telling me anything! Why should I trust you now?"

Alex flinched at her words, as if her anger was a physical blow. His gaze softened for a moment, but the tension in his jaw remained. He took a slow step toward her, as if trying to bridge the distance between them.

"I'm sorry," he murmured. "I never meant to put you in harm's way. You were never supposed to be part of this." He looked away briefly, his eyes darting to the photographs on the floor. "But I can't keep lying to you. I can't keep you in the dark any longer."

Zara's mind spun. She had always felt there was something off about him, something elusive about the man she had come to

The Revelation

care for, but this? This was something she hadn't expected. The danger, the secrecy, the people searching for him—it was all too much.

"Then tell me everything," Zara demanded, her voice sharp, desperate. "Tell me who you really are. What is all this? What do they want with you?"

Alex's eyes met hers again, and for the first time, Zara saw a flicker of something vulnerable in them—something raw. "You're right," he said, his voice barely above a whisper. "You deserve the truth. But it's not a simple story. And once you know, once you understand, there's no going back. You'll be involved, whether you want to be or not."

Zara took a deep breath, her heart pounding in her chest. She had no idea what she was about to hear, but she couldn't walk away from it now. Whatever Alex had been hiding, she needed to know. She needed to understand the man she had let into her life.

Alex took another step toward her, his gaze never leaving hers. "I'm not who you think I am, Zara. My name is Alex, yes. But that's about where the truth ends. I wasn't born into a normal life. My family—my real family—is involved in things that most people can't even begin to comprehend."

Zara's breath hitched. "What do you mean?" she asked, her voice barely audible. "What kind of things?"

Alex's eyes hardened as he spoke, his voice low, almost measured. "My family isn't just wealthy, Zara. We're part of something bigger. Something that's been in the shadows for generations. My father is a powerful figure in a network of global influence. We have ties to governments, corporations, criminal organizations. We pull strings in ways that most people would never even imagine."

Zara's mind reeled as she processed his words. It was too much to take in. She couldn't fathom what he was telling her. The man she had come to know, the man who had seemed so quiet and humble, was connected to something this dark? To people with this much power?

"Why didn't you tell me this?" Zara asked, her voice breaking slightly. "Why didn't you tell me who you really were?"

Alex's expression softened, but only for a moment. "I wanted to keep you safe. I wanted you to see me for who I was, not for who my family is. But the truth is, I've been running from this life for years. And I thought I could keep it separate. I thought I could stay away from it all, from the danger, the manipulation. But you... you became part of it. And that's when things got complicated."

Zara's thoughts were jumbled. She couldn't make sense of everything he was saying. It felt like a bad dream, like the life she had been living had suddenly twisted into something unrecognizable.

"What do you mean 'I became part of it'?" she asked, her voice rising with confusion. "What does that even mean?"

The Revelation

Alex ran a hand through his hair, his eyes flickering with uncertainty. "Because I brought you into this. Without meaning to. When I met you, I didn't realize how close I was to crossing a line. But I've been working against my family for a long time, Zara. I've been trying to dismantle what they've built. I didn't want you to be caught in the crossfire. I wanted you to think I was just another guy, someone you could have a normal relationship with."

Zara felt a sharp pang in her chest. She had always felt that something about Alex was too good to be true. But she never expected this. She never expected a life of power, control, and danger.

"So… these people who are looking for you? They're part of your family?" she asked, her voice trembling.

Alex nodded. "They're members of my family's organization. They're trying to force me back into the fold. They want me to take my place and help expand their reach, but I won't. I can't."

Zara's head spun as the pieces of the puzzle began to fall into place, though she didn't like the picture they were forming. She looked at Alex, searching his face for some sign that this was all a mistake, some indication that he wasn't telling her the full truth.

"Why didn't you just leave?" she whispered, her voice trembling with disbelief. "Why didn't you walk away from all of this? Why didn't you leave me out of it?"

Alex's gaze dropped, his shoulders slumping with an emotion that Zara couldn't read. "I tried. I really did. But when you came into my life... everything changed. I couldn't just walk away from you. You became too important to me. And that's why I couldn't risk dragging you into this. But it's too late. You're already involved."

Zara stood there, her mind reeling, the weight of his words pressing down on her. She felt betrayed, confused, and scared all at once. Everything she had believed about Alex—about their connection—was shattered in that instant. She had known him as a kind, caring man, someone she could trust. But now? Now, everything was different.

She took a shaky step back, her hands clutching at the edges of the table for support. "What do we do now?" she asked, her voice quiet but filled with fear.

Alex didn't answer immediately. Instead, he walked toward her, closing the distance between them. His eyes were filled with something—desperation, perhaps, or regret.

"We survive," he said, his voice low. "We survive, and we find a way to get out of this. Together."

But even as he said it, Zara couldn't shake the feeling that the life she had once known was slipping away. The world she had stepped into was far darker than she had ever imagined, and Alex, for all his promises, was already lost within it.

Seven

The Confrontation

Zara's hands were shaking, her pulse pounding in her ears. The truth—Alex's truth—had shattered everything she thought she knew about him. The world she had thought she was living in, a world of quiet cafés and intimate conversations, now felt like a distant memory. Now, nothing made sense. Nothing seemed safe. The man she had come to care for, to trust, had drawn her into a web of secrecy, power, and danger. And now, standing in the dimly lit warehouse, Zara was faced with the consequences.

Alex had promised her answers. He had sworn that they would get through this together, that they would find a way out. But the longer she stood there, watching him, the more she wondered if his promises were just another layer of deception.

"Alex," Zara's voice was trembling as she spoke, her words

slipping out in a rush. "I need to understand. I need you to explain this to me—everything. You can't just keep hiding things from me, not anymore. I'm already caught up in this mess. You can't protect me from the truth any longer."

Alex's eyes were stormy, his jaw clenched tight. His posture had shifted; no longer was he the vulnerable man who had looked to her for comfort. Now, he stood before her like a man caught between two worlds—one that he couldn't escape, and another that he wasn't ready to embrace.

"I never wanted you to get involved," he muttered, almost to himself. "I wanted you to have a life—your life. But you're right. I can't keep hiding this from you. I never should have dragged you into it."

Zara's heart ached as she looked at him, but anger bubbled up inside her, hot and sharp. "Dragged me into it? You think you dragged me into this? Alex, you didn't just drag me into this—you pulled me in, you showed me a side of yourself, made me trust you. And then when things started to get real, you shut me out. You disappeared. You left me in the dark."

Alex flinched, his eyes darkening. "I didn't leave you," he said, his voice tight. "I was trying to protect you."

Zara let out a bitter laugh, shaking her head. "Protect me? By lying to me? By keeping me in the dark about who you really are? By making me think you were just some normal guy? You think that's protecting me?"

The Confrontation

"I didn't know what else to do!" Alex's voice cracked as he stepped closer to her, his hands clenched by his sides. "I wanted to give you a chance at something real, something that wasn't tied to my family's legacy. I wanted you to love me, not the person they want me to be. But it's not that simple. You have no idea what they're capable of. If I didn't keep you at arm's length, they'd come for you. And I couldn't let that happen."

Zara's chest tightened at his words, the weight of his fears pressing down on her. "So, what? You thought lying was the answer? Keeping me at a distance, telling me nothing? You never even asked if I could handle the truth. You just decided for me."

"I didn't know how to tell you," Alex whispered, his voice cracking. "I didn't know how to explain that everything—everything I've been running from—was going to catch up with me eventually. And now it has. It's all coming for us, Zara. The men after me—they'll stop at nothing to get what they want. And they think they can use you to get to me."

Zara's heart skipped a beat. "Use me? For what? What do they want with me? I don't understand any of this, Alex. What kind of person are you?"

Alex's expression hardened, the vulnerability from moments ago disappearing behind a wall of resolve. "I'm the son of a man who controls more than you can imagine. My father is one of the most powerful men in the world. And everything—every decision, every move I've made—has been because of him and the empire he built. But I'm not like him. I never was. I wanted out, Zara. But the truth is, I can't escape it. They won't let me."

Zara stepped back, her mind reeling. "Your father? Is that what this is about? Your family is involved in something… something illegal, something dangerous, and you're caught in the middle of it?" Her voice trembled with disbelief. "You let me fall in love with you, and you didn't think to tell me any of this? You didn't think I deserved to know what you were really a part of?"

"I didn't want to hurt you," Alex said, his voice low. "I didn't want you to see me the way they do. As a tool. As a pawn."

"A pawn," Zara echoed, her voice catching in her throat. "That's how you see yourself? A pawn in their game?"

Alex's gaze dropped to the floor, his expression tight with frustration. "I didn't ask for this life. I never wanted it. But my family won't let me go. They want me to take my place in their world. To become a part of their empire. But I refuse. I've been trying to get out of it for years, Zara. I've been running from them. And every time I think I'm free, they pull me back in."

Zara stood there, her mind struggling to process everything he had just said. She had known Alex was hiding something. She had known that he wasn't just an ordinary man, that there was more to his story than he had let on. But this? This was more than she could have ever imagined. His family was powerful—dangerously so. And now, it seemed like they had found a way to drag her into their world, too.

"I didn't ask for any of this," Zara said, her voice shaking with

The Confrontation

emotion. "I didn't ask to be part of your world, Alex. You promised me honesty. You promised me that we could have something real. And now I find out that everything about you was a lie."

Alex's eyes flickered with pain at her words. "It wasn't a lie. It wasn't a lie that I care about you. That I want to be with you. But I was afraid, Zara. I was afraid that if I told you the truth, you'd walk away. I couldn't lose you."

Zara felt a lump form in her throat, the rawness in his voice tugging at her heart. She had believed in him, trusted him. But now, she was left questioning everything. Was any of it real? Was he just another part of his family's game?

"Why didn't you trust me?" she whispered, her voice breaking. "Why didn't you believe that I could handle it? Why didn't you believe that I could help you?"

Alex stepped toward her, his hand reaching out, but Zara recoiled instinctively. "Because you don't know what this world is like," he said urgently. "You don't know the danger you're in. If I brought you into this, they'd use you against me. And I can't let that happen."

"I am in this now," Zara shot back, her voice sharp. "You can't just push me away. You can't just shut me out. This is my life, too, now. You made it mine when you chose to pull me in. You can't undo it."

There was a long, tense silence. Alex stood there, his eyes locked onto hers, as though he was weighing something in his mind. Then, finally, he spoke, his voice low and filled with a sense of resignation.

"You're right," he said, his voice quiet but steady. "You're already involved. And I can't protect you from this anymore. But I will not let them use you against me. I won't let them hurt you. If I have to walk away from this—if I have to walk away from my family, my legacy, my empire—I'll do it. For you."

Zara's heart skipped a beat. "What are you saying?"

"I'm saying that I'll fight for you," Alex said, his gaze unwavering. "I'll do whatever it takes to protect you, even if it means giving up everything I've ever known."

Tears welled up in Zara's eyes as she took a step toward him. She had always believed in him, had always believed that he was more than his family, more than the dangerous world they had created for him. And now, as she looked at him, she knew that the stakes were higher than ever. They were both in too deep.

"Then we fight together," Zara said, her voice steady despite the whirlwind of emotions inside her. "We fight together, or we don't fight at all."

For a moment, neither of them spoke. The weight of their words hung between them, heavy with the understanding that there was no going back now. Whatever came next, they were in it together. And in that moment, Zara realized that she had made her choice. She had chosen Alex. And now, she had to face the consequences—whatever they might be.

"Together," Alex repeated, his voice hoarse but resolute.

And with that, the air between them shifted. What had once been a fragile bond of trust and hope now became something stronger—something born of necessity, of survival. They were no longer two people caught in a game of secrets and lies. They were two people who had crossed a line, and now they had to fight to stay alive in a world that wanted to tear them apart.

Eight

The Past Unveiled

Zara stood in the dimly lit room, her eyes locked on Alex as the weight of his words settled over her like a heavy fog. She had always thought of Alex as a mystery, but the man standing before her now was a stranger—one she had never truly known. He had shared fragments of his past, pieces of a life she could hardly comprehend, but now he was opening the door to that past, ready to reveal everything that had been hidden behind years of silence and deception.

Her heart pounded in her chest as she waited for him to speak, to explain the truth that she had demanded for so long. But even as she stood there, ready to hear whatever he had to say, a part of her was afraid. Afraid of what the truth might do to them. Afraid of what she might learn.

Alex took a deep breath, his eyes never leaving hers. His hands

The Past Unveiled

trembled slightly at his sides, betraying the calm facade he had worked so hard to maintain. It was clear to Zara that he had fought this moment for years—had run from it, hidden from it. And now, there was no choice but to face it head-on.

"You deserve to know everything," he said quietly, his voice rough with emotion. "You've been dragged into this whether you like it or not. And now, I can't protect you from the truth anymore."

Zara's heart raced as she stepped forward, trying to steady herself, to control the torrent of thoughts swirling in her mind. "Then tell me. Tell me everything, Alex. I'm not going to walk away from you, not now. But I need to understand. I need to know who you really are."

Alex swallowed hard, his jaw clenching as he looked away for a moment, as if gathering the courage to speak. When he finally met her eyes again, the pain in them was raw, exposed. It was the kind of pain that only came from years of secrets, years of running from the past. But now, there was no place left to hide.

"My father," Alex began, his voice low, almost hoarse. "He's not just some businessman or rich tycoon. He's a force in the world, Zara. A man whose influence stretches across continents, whose wealth is enough to control governments, industries, entire economies. And I was born into it. Into a life where everything was preordained, where every decision I made, every move I took, was part of a bigger plan—a plan I had no say in."

Zara's stomach twisted as she listened to him speak, the gravity of his words sinking in. She had known that Alex's family was powerful, but this? This was beyond anything she had imagined. She felt the ground beneath her feet shift as the world she thought she understood fell away.

"Did you ever have a choice?" she asked, her voice barely above a whisper.

Alex's eyes darkened, and for a moment, he didn't answer. His gaze drifted, distant, as if he were lost in the memories that threatened to consume him. "I thought I did. I thought I could walk away from it all. But you can't escape it when you're born into it. My father... he's ruthless. And he's been grooming me for years to take over. I was supposed to follow in his footsteps, to inherit everything he built. But I didn't want it. I didn't want any part of the life he wanted for me."

Zara felt a pang of sympathy, but it was quickly replaced by a wave of anger. "But you didn't tell me. You never told me the truth. You kept me in the dark, Alex. You made me think we had something real, something normal. And all this time, I've been living a lie."

"I never meant to lie to you," Alex said, his voice breaking. "I never meant to deceive you. I wanted you to have a life outside of all of this. I wanted you to love me, not the legacy I was born into. But I couldn't protect you from this world. I couldn't protect you from them."

Zara's breath caught in her throat as she looked at him. She could see the pain in his eyes, the weight of the past that he had carried for so long. But she couldn't ignore the anger bubbling up inside her. He had kept so much from her. He had kept her in the dark when she had trusted him.

"Who are they, Alex?" she demanded, her voice trembling with emotion. "Who are these people you're running from? What do they want with you? And why is it all tied to me?"

Alex hesitated, his eyes flickering with uncertainty. "My father's organization isn't just a business, Zara. It's a network. A secretive, powerful network with ties to everything—politicians, law enforcement, criminals, even military leaders. They control everything from behind the scenes. And my father, he's at the top. He's the one pulling the strings. The people after me—they're part of his plan to bring me back into the fold. To make me take my place in their world."

Zara's mind raced as she processed his words. This wasn't just about money. It wasn't just about power. This was a life Alex had been trying to escape—a life that had never been his choice. "And you were running from all of this? From your father? From them?"

"I tried," Alex said, his voice strained. "I tried to break free. I tried to live my own life. But it's not that simple. They always find a way back. They always pull me back in. I've been running for years, but I can't outrun my bloodline, Zara. I can't outrun what I was born into."

Zara's chest tightened as the pieces of the puzzle began to fall into place. The man she had trusted, the man she had come to care for, was trapped in a world of shadows and danger—a world he couldn't escape. And now, she was in the middle of it too. She was part of the equation now, whether she wanted to be or not.

"But why me?" Zara asked, her voice shaking. "Why bring me into this? Why make me a part of your world when you knew it would only bring danger?"

Alex stepped closer, his eyes filled with regret. "I never meant for you to get caught in this. I never wanted you to know. But when I met you—when I saw you—I couldn't stay away. I wanted something real, something that wasn't tied to all the lies and manipulation. You made me believe that it was possible. That I could have something normal. And I wanted to keep that. But I didn't realize how dangerous it would get. I didn't realize that they'd come after you too."

Zara's mind was spinning. She had always known that there was something about Alex that didn't quite add up, something hidden beneath the surface. But this? This was a world of darkness, of control, of power beyond anything she could have imagined. And now, she was entangled in it. She was part of this world, whether she liked it or not.

"I don't know what to believe anymore," Zara whispered, her voice cracking. "I don't know what's real. What if everything we had was just part of their game? What if they were controlling you the whole time? What if you were never really you?"

Alex's face twisted with guilt and pain, but he didn't back away.

The Past Unveiled

"I wasn't lying to you, Zara. I wasn't using you. I—I wanted you. I wanted to be with you. But I couldn't let you into the darkness of my world. I couldn't let you see what it was really like. And now, I've dragged you into it, and I don't know how to get you out."

Zara's chest tightened, her mind racing with the gravity of what he was saying. She had come to him for answers, for understanding, but now, everything felt like a lie. Every word, every moment they had shared, felt like a part of something bigger than either of them—something far more dangerous than she could have ever imagined.

"I want to believe you," she whispered, her eyes welling with tears. "But I don't know if I can."

Alex's hand reached out to touch her cheek, his fingers trembling as they grazed her skin. "I'm not asking you to forgive me. I'm asking you to believe that I never wanted to drag you into this. I never wanted you to be a part of my father's world. But it's too late now. We're both part of it."

The silence between them was thick with unspoken emotions, with the weight of everything Alex had shared. Zara felt her heart break in two, torn between the man she had come to love and the dangerous world he was trapped in. She had trusted him, had let him in, and now she was left with nothing but the wreckage of their lives, a life she never asked for, but one she could no longer escape.

The truth was out. The past had been unveiled. And there was no turning back now.

"I don't know what comes next, Alex," Zara said, her voice breaking. "But I know one thing. I won't let you face this alone."

Alex's eyes softened, his relief palpable. He pulled her into his arms, holding her tightly, as if he were afraid to let her go. And for the first time in a long time, Zara didn't pull away. She let herself be held, knowing that the road ahead would be long and dangerous, but knowing that, for better or for worse, they would face it together.

But the truth had been unveiled. And nothing would ever be the same again.

Nine

A Dangerous Rival

Zara sat in the dimly lit apartment, the soft hum of the city outside doing little to calm her racing thoughts. She hadn't slept in days—too many questions, too many unknowns swirling in her mind. Alex's confession, his painful unveiling of the past, had shattered everything she thought she understood about their relationship, about him, about the life she had been drawn into. She couldn't escape the nagging feeling that she was only beginning to scratch the surface of the world Alex had been hiding from her.

The truth had been too much to process at once. His father's empire, the dangerous web of power and influence Alex was entangled in, the promises of protection—Zara was left in a whirlwind of confusion. She had believed in him, had wanted to believe that the connection they shared was something real, something outside the dark world Alex had grown up in. But now, everything was muddied, uncertain. She couldn't shake the feeling that the worst was yet to come.

She stood up from the couch, pacing the small room, her mind trying to make sense of the chaos that had become her life. Alex had promised they would fight through this, together. But now, she wasn't so sure. How could they face this world—a world she didn't understand—if she didn't even know who she could trust? And even more, how could she trust Alex when it seemed like he was constantly running, hiding from something he couldn't escape?

Her thoughts were interrupted by the soft chime of her phone, the notification lighting up the dark room. Her heart skipped a beat as she saw the name on the screen: Alex. She picked up the phone, her fingers trembling as she answered.

"Zara," Alex's voice came through the speaker, tight and urgent. "I need you to listen to me carefully. You're not safe. They're coming for us. You need to leave. Now."

A cold chill ran down Zara's spine. She barely had time to process the words before Alex's voice continued, the rawness in it sending a ripple of dread through her.

"It's not just my family who's after me. There's someone else, someone much more dangerous. His name is Viktor. He's a rival. A man who wants to take everything my father has built—and he'll stop at nothing to get it. He's been after me for years. And now, he's targeting you."

A Dangerous Rival

Zara's breath caught in her throat. "Viktor?" Her voice trembled with confusion. "Who is he? Why are you so afraid of him?"

Alex's voice grew more strained. "Viktor is ruthless. He's been trying to take control of the empire for years, and he sees me as a threat. But it's worse than that—he's been using my father's influence to manipulate things in his favor. He's not just a businessman. He's dangerous, unpredictable. And now, he's decided to make his move. He knows about you, Zara. And that makes you a target."

Zara's heart pounded in her chest. The walls of her apartment felt like they were closing in on her. Viktor. She had heard whispers of men like him—powerful, untouchable men who played games in the shadows, whose wealth and influence bent the world to their will. But now, it wasn't just a story. It wasn't just a rumor. It was real. It was happening. And she was right in the middle of it.

"I don't understand," she whispered, the words barely escaping her lips. "Why me? What does he want with me?"

Alex's voice was firm, though tinged with desperation. "Viktor isn't after you for who you are, Zara. He's after you because you're tied to me. He knows I won't let him have the empire without a fight, and now, he's trying to hurt me by going after you. He wants to destroy everything I care about—starting with you."

Zara felt a wave of nausea rise in her chest. She couldn't believe what she was hearing. This wasn't the world she had ever wanted to be a part of. She wasn't ready for this kind of danger, this kind of uncertainty. But now, there was no turning back. She was already a part of it. She was already in too deep.

"You have to leave," Alex's voice broke through her thoughts. "Pack your things and go somewhere safe. I'll come for you, but you need to get out of there now."

Before Zara could respond, the line went dead. She stared at the phone in her hand, her heart thundering in her chest. She had no idea what was happening, no idea what kind of danger she was facing, but one thing was clear: the world Alex had tried so hard to keep her away from had found her. And now, there was no escape.

—-

Zara stood in the middle of her apartment, her hands trembling as she packed a bag. Clothes, toiletries, anything she could grab in a hurry. Her mind was racing, each thought crashing into the next. What should she do? Where should she go? She couldn't just run blindly; she needed to think. She needed a plan.

Her mind kept returning to the same thing: Viktor. The man Alex had warned her about. The man who was now hunting her. She didn't know what he wanted, or why he was so obsessed with taking down Alex, but one thing was certain—he was dangerous. And she had no idea how to fight back against someone like that.

She glanced at her phone again, hoping to see a message or a call from Alex, but there was nothing. The silence was suffocating. Was he alright? Was he already on his way? Or was Viktor's reach already too far? The uncertainty gnawed at her, and every second felt like an eternity.

Her thoughts were interrupted by the sound of a knock on her door. Zara froze, her heart skipping a beat. She wasn't expecting anyone. She hadn't told anyone she was leaving. Could it be him? Could it be Viktor's men already here?

She stepped quietly toward the door, her hand brushing against the knife she had grabbed from the kitchen earlier. It wasn't much, but it was something. She wasn't prepared for a fight. But she wouldn't go down without one.

She peered through the peephole, her breath catching in her throat when she saw who was standing on the other side. It wasn't Viktor. It wasn't anyone she knew. It was a man—a tall, well-dressed figure who stood with an air of authority that sent a shiver down her spine. He was watching her door, waiting. And somehow, she knew he wasn't here to deliver good news.

Zara's mind raced. Was he one of Viktor's men? Or worse, was he part of Alex's father's network—someone sent to keep her under control, to stop her from running? She had no way of knowing. But one thing was certain: she couldn't take any chances.

Her hand hovered over the door handle. She needed to act quickly, to make a decision. She couldn't wait around for the answers to come to her.

The Wealth Beneath Her Struggles

Taking a deep breath, Zara stepped back from the door, her heart pounding in her chest. She grabbed her phone, quickly dialing Alex's number, praying he would answer.

It rang once, twice. Then, the line clicked, and Alex's voice came through, strained and urgent.

"Zara? Where are you? What happened? I told you to leave!"

"I'm still here. I don't know what to do, Alex. There's someone at my door. I don't know who they are, but they're waiting. I think they're here for me."

Alex's voice cracked through the line. "Listen to me. You have to leave. Don't open the door. Don't trust anyone who knocks. I'll be there soon, but you need to get out now."

Zara's pulse quickened. She looked back at the door, the figure still standing there, unmoving. She could feel the weight of his presence through the door, like a threat she couldn't escape.

"I don't know if I can get away," she whispered, her voice trembling. "I don't know where to go. I don't know who I can trust."

Alex's voice softened, but it was firm. "You can trust me, Zara. And I'm coming for you. But you need to survive long enough for me to get there. Stay hidden. Stay quiet. Don't let him in."

Zara felt a lump form in her throat as she clutched the phone tighter. "Okay. I'll wait for you. But please hurry, Alex. Please."

A Dangerous Rival

She hung up the phone, her heart racing. She knew she had to be careful. One wrong move, and everything Alex had tried to protect her from would come crashing down. But as she stood there, staring at the door, she knew one thing for certain: Viktor wasn't the only danger lurking in the shadows. The real question was whether Alex could get to her in time, or if she would be caught in the crossfire between two dangerous forces—forces she couldn't even begin to understand.

Ten

A Test of Trust

The night was too still. Zara sat on the edge of the bed, her hands clutching the edges of the blanket as she stared out the window. The city below seemed to pulse with a quiet rhythm, the glow of streetlights casting long shadows across the empty streets. Everything felt so distant now—so far removed from the life she had known. She had been running from something for so long, something she couldn't understand. And now, as the minutes ticked by, as she waited for Alex, she realized she was running from him too.

It was a thought she had been avoiding all evening. But now, with the silence stretching on, it seemed impossible to ignore. Could she trust him? After everything he had told her, everything that had been hidden from her, could she still believe in the man she had come to care for? He had promised her answers, but all he had given her was more uncertainty,

A Test of Trust

more confusion. Viktor, his father's empire, the dangerous world they were both entangled in—it was all too much.

Her phone lay next to her, its screen cracked from when she had dropped it earlier, but it still worked. She hadn't heard from Alex since their last conversation, and the silence only heightened her anxiety. Where was he? Why hadn't he come for her? Had Viktor's men found him already? The thoughts swirled, each one more terrifying than the last.

Zara stood up, pacing the small room, her mind racing with questions. Every sound, every flicker of light, made her jump, her nerves on edge. She couldn't sit still any longer. She needed to know what was happening. She needed to understand what Alex had dragged her into.

A knock at the door.

Her body stiffened, and she froze. Her breath caught in her throat. The knock was too soft to be an emergency, too measured to be someone threatening. But she didn't know who it was. She couldn't afford to trust anyone.

Zara's hand moved instinctively toward the knife she had kept by the door for protection. She wasn't naïve. Not anymore. She had learned that the world she thought she understood was a lie, a façade hiding something much darker, much more dangerous.

The knock came again, this time louder, more insistent. But there was something familiar about it. Something that made her hesitate.

"Zara," a voice called from the other side, muffled through the door. "It's me. Alex."

Her heart skipped a beat, and for a split second, everything seemed to stop. It couldn't be him. He was supposed to be on his way. He had promised he would come. But there was no way to know for sure. Could it really be him?

"Alex?" Zara's voice cracked as she spoke, her mind racing. "Is that really you?"

There was a long pause, and then Alex's voice came again, this time sharper, more urgent. "Zara, please, open the door. We don't have much time. They're coming."

The sound of his voice, the urgency in it, broke through the haze of doubt in her mind. It had to be him. No one else knew her name, no one else knew where she was. She had to trust him. She had no choice.

But even as she moved toward the door, as her hand reached for the handle, doubt gnawed at her. This wasn't just about her safety anymore. This was about everything—about the lies, the secrets, the dangerous game Alex had dragged her into. Could she trust him? Could she trust the man who had kept so much from her, who had pulled her into a world of shadows and lies?

Zara hesitated for one more moment, her hand resting on the door. Her mind screamed at her to stay safe, to keep the

A Test of Trust

door closed, to protect herself from whatever danger Alex was bringing with him. But in the end, it wasn't fear that moved her—it was something deeper, something that had been there from the moment they met. It was trust. A trust she wasn't sure she could explain, but one that had always been there, even in the darkest moments.

She opened the door.

Alex stood there, just as she remembered, but there was something different about him now. His clothes were disheveled, his face lined with exhaustion. He looked like a man who had been running, who had been fighting a battle he couldn't win. His eyes locked onto hers, and for a brief moment, everything else disappeared. The chaos, the danger—it all seemed to fade as their eyes met.

"Zara," he said softly, his voice breaking the silence. "I'm sorry. I'm so sorry I made you wait. I didn't want you to see any of this. I never wanted you to be part of this world, but it's too late now. You're already in it."

Zara's throat tightened, and the words she had been holding in all night finally slipped out. "You promised me, Alex. You promised that you'd be honest. But all you've done is lie to me. I don't know who you are anymore."

Alex's eyes darkened, a flicker of pain passing through them. "I never meant to lie to you. But I had no choice. I couldn't bring you into this. I couldn't bring you into my family's world. But you're already here. You're already caught in it."

Zara shook her head, her emotions swirling. She wanted to believe him. She wanted to trust him. But she couldn't ignore the feeling that something was wrong, that he was still hiding something. The silence between them stretched on, heavy with unspoken words.

"What do you want from me, Alex?" she whispered. "What do you want me to do? You've dragged me into this mess, and now you're telling me I'm supposed to trust you? How can I do that?"

Alex stepped forward, his eyes never leaving hers. "You don't have to trust me. But I need you to believe in what we have. I need you to believe that we can make it through this, together. You're not just some pawn in this game, Zara. You're part of this fight now. And if we're going to survive, we need to trust each other. No matter what happens."

Zara's breath hitched as she looked at him, her mind a whirlwind of confusion and fear. She didn't know if she could trust him. She didn't know if she could trust anyone anymore. But one thing was clear: she couldn't walk away. Not now. Not after everything they had been through.

She took a deep breath, her voice trembling. "Okay. I'll trust you. But if anything happens to me, Alex—if anything happens to us—I won't forgive you."

Alex's face softened, and for the first time in what felt like forever, a flicker of hope crossed his eyes. "You have my word, Zara. I'll protect you. I swear it."

A Test of Trust

Before Zara could say another word, the sound of heavy footsteps echoed down the hallway. Someone was coming. She could hear the muffled voices of men, their words indistinguishable but filled with a sense of purpose. Alex's eyes widened, and without a word, he grabbed her hand, pulling her toward the back of the apartment.

"They found us," Alex said urgently, his grip tightening around her wrist. "They know where we are. We don't have much time."

Zara's heart raced as she followed him, her mind reeling with the realization that the world they were running from had finally caught up to them. She had trusted him. She had opened the door, opened her heart, and now she had to trust that he would protect her, that he would keep his promise.

They reached the back door, and Alex shoved it open, glancing back one last time to make sure Zara was right behind him. "Stay close," he muttered, his voice steady despite the danger closing in on them. "I'll get you out of here."

Zara's pulse hammered in her ears as they moved down the narrow alley behind the building, the cold air biting at her skin. Every step felt like it was taking them further away from everything they had once known, from everything that had once felt safe.

But there was no turning back. Not now. Not when everything was on the line.

The sound of footsteps grew louder behind them, and Zara's breath caught in her throat. They were close. Too close.

Alex glanced over his shoulder, his expression grim. "We have to move faster."

As they rounded the corner, a black car screeched to a halt in front of them. The doors flew open, and men in suits stepped out, their faces cold and emotionless. Viktor's men. Zara could see the gleam of weapons tucked beneath their jackets, their eyes scanning the alley, searching for any sign of movement.

Alex's grip tightened around her hand as they both turned to run, the sound of the men's footsteps echoing behind them, chasing them, closing in.

Zara's heart pounded in her chest as they sprinted down the alley, the world around them blurring into a haze of motion. She didn't know where they were going, didn't know what was happening, but she couldn't stop running. She couldn't stop now.

Her mind screamed with questions. Could she trust Alex? Could she trust him to get them out of this alive?

But in that moment, all she knew was that she had to trust him. There was no other choice.

The chase had begun. And they were running out of time.

Eleven

The Unraveling

The night air was thick with tension, and the quiet sounds of the city felt like a distant hum in Zara's ears as she sprinted down the alleyway, Alex just a few steps ahead. Her lungs burned, her legs heavy from the effort, but she pushed on, the sound of footsteps behind them growing louder with each passing second. She could hear the faint echo of voices—men calling out in harsh whispers, instructions being barked with urgency.

Viktor's men were closing in, and the fear gripping Zara's chest seemed to grow tighter with every heartbeat. She didn't know where she was running to, didn't know what kind of escape Alex had in mind, but she couldn't afford to think too much about it. Her mind was a whirlwind of questions, doubt, and panic. Where was Alex leading her? What had he gotten them into? And what would happen when they caught up with them?

Alex's grip on her hand never loosened, pulling her along with a sense of urgency that mirrored her own rising panic. He glanced over his shoulder every few moments, his face hard with determination, his eyes scanning the darkness ahead. His focus never wavered. Despite the chaos surrounding them, Alex seemed to know exactly where they were going.

But Zara didn't. She didn't know who to trust anymore—who Alex really was, or whether any of the promises he had made were even real. She had believed in him once, but now she wondered if she had ever truly known the man who had come into her life so unexpectedly, who had woven a story of protection and care, only to reveal that it was all tangled in lies, deception, and danger.

They turned another corner, and Alex pulled her into a small alcove behind a row of dumpsters. His grip on her wrist tightened, his breathing heavy as he glanced around them, his eyes darting to the shadows. Zara could feel her heart pounding in her chest as she tried to steady her breath, tried to quell the rising tide of fear in her gut.

"This way," Alex whispered urgently, pushing her toward a narrow side street. He didn't wait for her to answer, just pulled her along again, his eyes flickering nervously as they moved.

Zara's mind was a jumble of conflicting emotions. She was terrified, of course. But there was something else—a growing sense of betrayal that gnawed at her insides. She didn't know if Alex was the man he had claimed to be anymore. Everything had felt so real when they were together—the late-

The Unraveling

night conversations, the quiet moments shared between them. But now, she wasn't so sure.

She thought back to their first meeting, the way Alex had seemed so kind, so unassuming. He had seemed like the kind of man who could lead her to something better. But now, as they moved deeper into the night, into the shadows, she couldn't help but wonder if she had just been another pawn in his game. Had he ever really cared about her? Or had she just been an obstacle to be manipulated, a means to an end?

"Zara, stay focused," Alex's voice cut through her thoughts. "We need to keep moving. They're getting closer."

Zara nodded, though her mind was still spinning. She couldn't afford to let her doubt cloud her actions. Not now. Not with Viktor's men so close. But how long could she keep running from the truth? How long could she trust a man who had kept so many secrets from her? A man whose very existence seemed tied to a world of danger and corruption?

They reached another darkened corner, and Alex pressed his back against the wall, his breathing ragged as he peered around the edge, searching for any sign of movement. Zara stood beside him, her hand still in his, her pulse racing. They were both trapped in a game neither of them had chosen, both caught in a world that neither of them understood completely.

"I'm sorry, Zara," Alex said suddenly, his voice barely above a whisper. "I know I haven't been honest with you. I never wanted to drag you into this world. But now that you're in it... there's no way out."

Zara's breath hitched, the weight of his words sinking in. He had said something like that before. That there was no way out. But now, in the quiet darkness of this alley, with their lives hanging in the balance, the gravity of his statement felt heavier than it ever had.

"No way out?" Zara repeated, her voice trembling. She pulled back slightly, staring at him, her hand slipping from his grip. "Is that why you kept me in the dark? Because you thought I wouldn't understand? Or was it because you knew I wouldn't trust you if I knew what you were really a part of?"

Alex's face twisted with regret, his eyes flickering with something that looked like guilt. "Zara... I wanted to protect you. I didn't want you to get caught in the crossfire. But it's too late for that now. Viktor... he won't stop until he has everything. And he'll use you to get to me. He'll do anything."

"I don't care about Viktor!" Zara snapped, her frustration boiling over. "I care about you. And right now, I don't know if I can trust you anymore, Alex."

His eyes darkened, and for a moment, Zara saw a flicker of something she hadn't seen before. Anger. It was brief, but it was there. Then, just as quickly, it was gone, replaced by the same familiar mask of determination. He reached for her again, this time his touch gentler, more pleading.

"Zara," he said, his voice low. "I'm not asking you to trust me blindly. But right now, you don't have a choice. Viktor's men are closing in. We don't have much time. Please, just... trust me for one more night. One more night, and I'll explain everything. Everything I couldn't before."

Zara stood there for a long moment, her mind a storm of conflicting emotions. Part of her wanted to walk away, wanted to tell him that it was too late for promises. But another part of her, the part that still cared about him, still believed in what they had shared, knew that she couldn't leave him. Not now. Not when everything was coming apart.

"Okay," she said finally, her voice barely above a whisper. "One more night. But after this... you tell me everything. No more secrets, no more lies. I need to know who you really are."

Alex's face softened at her words, and for the first time in what felt like forever, a genuine smile tugged at his lips. "I promise, Zara. After tonight, you'll know everything."

They stayed in the shadows for what felt like hours, moving through alleyways and hidden side streets, always staying one step ahead of Viktor's men. Every so often, Zara would catch a glimpse of the dark figures in the distance, their faces hidden in the shadows, their footsteps echoing through the night. The tension in the air was suffocating, but Alex never wavered, his movements calculated, sure. He seemed to know exactly where they were going, exactly what needed to be done.

But as the night wore on, the truth began to settle over Zara like a heavy weight. She had trusted Alex. She had trusted him with her heart, with her life, and now she didn't know if that trust had been misplaced. She didn't know if she was part of a bigger plan, a game she couldn't see, or if she was still just a pawn in a game between two powerful forces. Viktor and Alex's father. Men who controlled the world from behind closed doors, who pulled strings without ever touching them.

And Alex… Alex had promised her everything. But had he ever really been honest with her?

They stopped in front of a small, unmarked door, hidden behind a row of old storage units. Alex knocked three times, quick and deliberate, before stepping back and looking at Zara. His expression was unreadable, but there was something in his eyes—something deep—that made her stomach churn.

"Inside," he said quietly. "We're safe for now. But you'll need to trust me, Zara. You'll need to trust that I'm doing everything I can to get us out of this."

Zara nodded, though her mind was still reeling. As she stepped inside the building, the door closed behind them with a soft click. They were alone again, the quiet of the room pressing in around them.

For the first time in what felt like forever, Zara looked at Alex and saw him—truly saw him—for who he was. Not the man who had tried to shield her from the darkness, not the man who had promised her safety. But the man who was caught in a web of lies, a man who had tried to outrun the legacy of his family, only to be dragged back into it.

The Unraveling

The truth was beginning to unravel, and with it came the realization that nothing, not even Alex, could protect her from the danger that was closing in. The game was changing, and the rules were becoming clearer. But the real question was whether they could survive the unraveling—or if it would tear them apart.

Twelve

The Breaking Point

The warehouse was suffocating.

Zara paced in the dimly lit space, her mind a battlefield. The walls felt as though they were closing in on her, pressing her from all sides. The once familiar hum of the city outside now seemed like a distant memory, far removed from the tense reality that surrounded her. She had always thought of herself as someone who could handle chaos, someone who could stay calm when the world seemed to spin out of control. But now, as she stood in the cold silence of the warehouse, she felt like she was drowning.

Alex had promised her that he would explain everything—that after the night was over, she would finally understand why he had kept so many secrets from her. But here she was, trapped in the dark, her heart heavy with doubt. Every step she had taken in this world, every choice she had made, had led her to this point. And now, she wasn't sure which way to turn.

The door creaked behind her, and Zara's heart leapt into her throat. She spun around, only to find Alex standing in the doorway, his face drawn, his expression tense.

"Zara," he said softly, his voice low and filled with regret. "We don't have much time. They're getting closer."

Zara stared at him, her chest tightening with a mixture of frustration and fear. She wanted to believe him, wanted to trust that he was doing everything he could to protect her, but the truth was, she wasn't sure what to believe anymore. The more Alex spoke, the more her doubts grew, like dark tendrils wrapping around her heart, choking the trust she had once had for him.

"I thought you said you were getting us out of this," she said, her voice barely above a whisper, tinged with anger. "I thought you said I would be safe."

Alex's eyes softened, but the weariness in them only deepened. "I never wanted this for you," he said, stepping into the room. "I never wanted to drag you into my world, Zara. But you're already part of it. And now, I have to protect you. I have to make sure you don't get caught in the crossfire."

Zara's mind raced. He had said something like that before, but this time, the words felt hollow. She had heard promises before—promises of protection, of safety—but they had all been shattered. Every promise he made seemed to come with strings attached, with a price that she wasn't sure she was willing to pay anymore.

"What am I supposed to do, Alex?" she asked, her voice trembling with emotion. "How can I trust you when everything you've told me feels like a lie?"

Alex's face twisted with a mixture of pain and guilt. He reached out, his hand brushing against hers, but Zara pulled away, her heart pounding in her chest. She couldn't let herself get pulled back in, not now. Not when she had come so close to understanding the truth.

"I'm not asking you to trust me blindly," Alex said, his voice shaking slightly. "But I'm asking you to trust that I'm trying to protect you. I'm trying to keep you safe, even if it means I have to lose everything."

Zara's eyes narrowed. "Everything? What do you mean by everything? What are you willing to lose, Alex?"

Alex opened his mouth as though to speak, but then stopped, his expression hardening. He clenched his fists at his sides, his jaw tight with frustration. "I'm willing to lose my family, my name, everything I've ever known, if it means you're safe. But it's not that simple. Viktor is coming. He's going to take everything I've built, and he's not going to stop until he gets it."

Zara's breath caught in her throat at the mention of Viktor's name. She had heard the rumors, the whispers of the man who was Alex's rival—the man who wanted to tear everything down, to seize control of the empire Alex had been born into. But this was different. Viktor wasn't just a distant threat anymore. He was here. He was coming for them.

"You think I don't know that?" Zara snapped, her frustration boiling over. "I've been running, hiding, pretending this isn't happening. But it is. I can't pretend anymore, Alex. I can't pretend that I'm not scared, that I'm not drowning in all the lies you've fed me. And now—now I have to face Viktor's men, too?"

Alex took a step forward, his expression softening. "Zara, please," he said, his voice thick with emotion. "I never wanted any of this for you. I never wanted you to be caught in this war between me and my father, between me and Viktor. But it's too late. You're already in it. And now, all I can do is fight for you, fight to get you out of this alive."

Zara's heart wrenched as she looked at him, her mind a whirlwind of conflicting emotions. She could see the sincerity in his eyes, the rawness of his words, but there was something else—something she couldn't ignore. He had kept so much from her. He had lied, manipulated, made promises he couldn't keep. How could she trust him now?

"You keep saying that you're doing this for me," she said, her voice breaking. "But what if it's not enough? What if we're too far gone? What if everything you've done has already doomed us?"

Alex's face hardened, the vulnerability that had flickered in his eyes replaced by a steely resolve. "Then we fight. We fight until the end, Zara. We don't give up."

Zara took a step back, her chest tightening with a mixture of fear and anger. "You want me to keep fighting for something that's already broken?" she asked, her voice rising. "You want me to keep running, to keep pretending that everything will work out, when we both know it's falling apart?"

"I'm not asking you to pretend!" Alex shouted, his voice shaking with emotion. "I'm asking you to trust me one last time. We have one shot at this. And if we fail… then we fail together. But I won't let you go down alone."

The words hung between them, heavy with the weight of everything they had been through. Zara felt as though the ground beneath her was crumbling, as though she was standing on the edge of a precipice, with nothing but darkness below. She had trusted him. She had believed in him. But now, the cracks in their relationship were too wide, too deep to ignore. How could she trust him when everything she knew about him had been a lie?

"I don't know if I can do this anymore, Alex," Zara whispered, her voice barely audible. "I don't know if I can keep pretending that everything will be okay when it's not."

Alex's face twisted with pain, his eyes flickering with the intensity of his emotions. He took a step toward her, but this time, she didn't back away. Instead, she stood her ground, her heart pounding in her chest as she looked into his eyes—eyes that she once thought she could trust, eyes that now felt like a stranger's.

"I'm sorry," Alex said, his voice cracking. "I'm sorry I couldn't give you the life you wanted. I'm sorry for all the pain I caused. But if there's one thing I know… it's that I can't lose you. Not now. Not after everything."

Zara's chest tightened as she fought back the tears that threatened to spill over. She had never felt so torn, so trapped between two worlds, two lives, neither of which she could fully embrace. She had come to love him, to trust him, but now she didn't know if she could continue to live in the shadow of his lies, in the suffocating grip of the world he had brought her into.

"I can't keep doing this, Alex," she whispered, her voice breaking. "I can't keep pretending that everything will be fine when it feels like we're falling apart."

Alex's eyes widened, the realization hitting him like a punch to the gut. "Zara…" He reached for her again, his hand trembling as he tried to close the distance between them. But she stepped back, shaking her head.

"I need space," she said softly, her voice steady despite the storm of emotions raging inside her. "I need to figure out who I am in all of this. I need to understand what I'm fighting for."

Alex stood there, his face pale, his expression a mixture of desperation and defeat. "Zara, please," he pleaded. "Don't walk away from me. Don't walk away from us."

But Zara couldn't hear him anymore. She had heard enough. The world around them was collapsing, and the trust she had once placed in Alex was slipping through her fingers like sand. She had tried to hold on, tried to make sense of it all, but now, as the weight of everything pressed down on her, she knew that this was the breaking point. And there was no turning back.

"I'm sorry," Zara whispered, her voice barely audible. She turned and walked away, the door clicking softly behind her, leaving Alex standing in the silence of his own broken promises.

Thirteen

A Risky Gamble

The heavy hum of the city outside felt distant as Zara sat in the cramped room, her eyes locked on the dimly lit corner. The silence was oppressive, suffocating. She could still feel the weight of the words they had exchanged, the sting of the anger that had built between her and Alex. He had gone silent after she walked away. He hadn't called, hadn't tried to reach her again. It felt as though they were living in two separate worlds now, worlds that could never intersect again. She had made her choice. At least, that was what she told herself.

But in her gut, there was a gnawing feeling—a feeling that wouldn't let her breathe easy. She couldn't shake the thought that she had abandoned him when he needed her most. The man she loved, the man she had trusted, was out there alone, running from Viktor and his men, while she cowered in a dark corner, too afraid to face the world they had been thrown into.

Zara reached for her phone, running her fingers over the cracked screen as she stared at it. It had been hours since she had last heard from Alex, and the quiet between them now felt like a silence too loud to ignore. She hated the uncertainty, hated the distance she had created. But how could she go back to him after everything? How could she go back and pretend that the past few days hadn't shattered the trust they once shared?

Her thumb hovered over Alex's contact, but just as she was about to dial, there was a knock at the door.

Zara's heart skipped a beat. She didn't know who it could be. Her apartment was on the fringes of the city, far enough away from the hustle and bustle to offer a sense of safety. But lately, she had felt like a target. Like someone was always watching, waiting for the right moment to strike. Her body tensed instinctively, and she reached for the knife she had kept near the door ever since Viktor's men had first shown up.

Another knock, this one louder and more insistent.

Zara's mind raced. She couldn't stay hidden forever. She couldn't live in fear, constantly waiting for the next threat to come. And yet, she didn't feel ready to face whatever danger was on the other side of that door.

Taking a deep breath, Zara crossed the room and peered through the peephole. Her breath caught in her throat. It was Alex. His face was gaunt, his eyes wild with desperation, but

A Risky Gamble

it was unmistakably him. Her heart ached at the sight of him. The man who had become her world was standing on the other side of the door, and all the anger, all the pain she had carried, melted away at the sight of him.

Without thinking, she swung the door open, and before she could say anything, Alex stepped inside, his eyes scanning the room as if he feared being followed. He didn't speak at first, only glanced at her for a long moment, as if trying to make sure she was really there, that she hadn't vanished like the other pieces of his life had.

"I didn't know where else to go," Alex said, his voice rough, almost hoarse. "I need your help, Zara. Please."

Zara felt the air around them shift, a tension between them that had been building for hours, maybe even longer. She didn't know whether she should be relieved, or angry, or terrified. But there was one thing she knew for certain: she couldn't turn him away.

"What happened?" she asked, her voice trembling despite herself. "Why are they after you? What's going on, Alex?"

He sighed, running a hand through his hair, his eyes dark with exhaustion. He looked every bit the part of a man who had been running for his life, and it wasn't just his outward appearance that betrayed his fear—it was the look in his eyes. It was a look Zara had seen before, in people who had nothing left to lose.

"Viktor," he said, the name falling from his lips like a curse. "He's moved faster than I expected. I thought I had more time. But he's been planning this for years, Zara. And now he's closing in on me. On us."

Zara stepped back, her mind racing. She had heard of Viktor. Everyone had. He was ruthless, unpredictable, a man with a thirst for power that knew no boundaries. But this? This was beyond anything she had imagined. She had thought that Alex was the one in control, the one who was running the show, pulling the strings. But now, it seemed as though they were all just pawns in Viktor's game.

"Then what do we do?" Zara asked, her voice barely above a whisper. "How do we stop him? How do we even fight him?"

Alex met her gaze, his eyes filled with something she couldn't quite decipher. There was fear, yes. But there was also something else—something colder. A hard edge, the kind of determination that made Zara wonder just how far Alex was willing to go to survive.

"We fight back," he said, his voice steady but filled with an urgency that sent a chill through her. "We don't run. We don't hide. I've spent my whole life running from my family, from Viktor, from this empire. But I'm done running. We're going to take the fight to him. We're going to beat him at his own game."

Zara felt a shiver run down her spine. She had known Alex was capable of anything, but this? This was a different side of him—one she wasn't sure she was ready to see. Was he willing to sacrifice everything for the sake of survival? Would he go so

A Risky Gamble

far that even she couldn't follow him?

"Alex..." Zara whispered, her voice shaking. "Are you sure? What if we can't win? What if it's too much? What if we're just setting ourselves up for disaster?"

Alex's eyes softened, and for a moment, Zara could see the vulnerability beneath the hardened exterior. "I don't know if we can win, Zara. I don't know if we can beat Viktor. But I can't let him destroy everything. Not again. Not like this."

Zara could feel her heart pounding in her chest. She was scared. She was terrified of the consequences of this decision, of what would happen if they failed. But at the same time, she knew that there was no turning back. There was no running away from this fight. And if they were going to do it, if they were going to face Viktor and his army of shadows, they would have to do it together.

She nodded, her breath shaky, but her voice steady. "Okay. We fight."

Alex's face softened, the tension in his shoulders easing as if a weight had been lifted. But there was still something in his eyes—something deep and dark that Zara couldn't ignore. She could see that he was gambling everything now. His life, his future, even her safety. And as much as she hated the thought of it, she knew that the only way to move forward was to trust him.

"I'll do whatever it takes to protect you," Alex said, his voice low and filled with conviction. "I'll risk everything to keep you safe, Zara. But this won't be easy. We need to move fast. We need to be prepared for anything."

Zara took a deep breath, trying to steady herself. She had trusted him once. She had fallen for him before, and despite all the doubts, all the questions swirling in her mind, she knew she had to trust him again. There was no other choice.

"Where do we start?" she asked, her voice steady now.

Alex turned toward the table, pulling out a map of the city. His fingers traced a series of lines, marking out key locations. "Viktor's been building his network for years. But I know where he's vulnerable. I know his weaknesses. And we're going to use them."

Zara leaned over the table, her eyes scanning the map. She could feel the adrenaline starting to course through her veins, the weight of the situation pressing in on her. They were about to take a risk—one that could either destroy them or change the course of everything. And yet, as she looked at Alex, there was something in his gaze that told her he wasn't backing down. He wasn't going to stop, no matter what.

She swallowed hard, her heart pounding. "Then let's do it."

And just like that, they were in it together. No more running. No more hiding. This was their fight. And nothing would ever be the same again.

Fourteen

The Final Test

The air was thick with tension as Zara and Alex crouched behind a stack of crates, their bodies pressed close together, their breaths shallow and synchronized. Their hands were sweaty from the tight grip they maintained on their weapons, fingers brushing with the raw, urgent connection of people who knew they were on the edge of something too big to ignore. The city buzzed behind them, but here, in the shadowed corner of the abandoned warehouse, everything felt eerily quiet. It was the calm before the storm.

Zara's heart beat in her chest, a drum of anticipation. It had all led to this—every decision, every betrayal, every moment of fear and uncertainty. The game had escalated. Viktor had made his move, and now, they were finally standing at the precipice, prepared to face him head-on. There was no going back. This was the final test.

The Wealth Beneath Her Struggles

She glanced at Alex, whose face was a mask of concentration, his jaw clenched, eyes scanning the darkened room where the shadows danced like ghosts. His posture was rigid, tense as if waiting for a storm to break, and Zara could feel the same storm swirling inside her. She wasn't sure if it was fear or the adrenaline coursing through her veins, but she knew this moment would determine everything.

They were about to take the fight directly to Viktor.

"Ready?" Alex's voice was quiet, but it carried an urgency that sent a shiver down Zara's spine.

Zara nodded, her breath shaky but her resolve steady. "Ready as I'll ever be."

Alex's lips barely parted in a semblance of a smile, but his eyes never left the center of the warehouse. He was always calculating, always ten steps ahead. It was what had made him so dangerous in the game they had been forced to play, and it was what had kept them alive this long.

"We can't hesitate," Alex said, his voice low and unwavering. "Viktor won't show mercy. Not to you, not to me. We end this now, or it ends us."

The words hung in the air, heavy with the weight of their truth. Zara swallowed hard, trying to calm her racing pulse. She had been in situations like this before, in the shadows, waiting for danger to strike. But something about this felt different. The stakes were higher. The consequences were beyond anything

The Final Test

she had ever faced. They were going up against a man who could topple empires with a single move, someone whose ruthlessness had no boundaries. And they were doing it with no guarantees, no backup, and no idea what Viktor might be capable of when cornered.

Zara glanced at Alex again. His dark, stormy eyes met hers, and for a moment, everything else faded. It was just the two of them, bound together by necessity, by the dangerous game they had both been forced into. She had trusted him, despite everything. Despite the lies, the manipulations, and the web of deceit he had pulled her into. And now, she had no choice but to trust him again.

They both knew the rules of this world—the rules that had governed Alex's life since birth. The rules of power, control, and survival. The rules that Viktor played by. In this world, there were no guarantees. Trust was fleeting, and betrayal was a currency just as valuable as loyalty.

Alex motioned for her to follow him as they moved through the darkened expanse of the warehouse. The air smelled of rust and oil, the space echoing with the sound of their footsteps as they made their way toward the center of the building. There was no turning back now. They had crossed a line, and the only option left was to push forward.

Suddenly, the silence shattered.

A loud crash echoed from the far side of the warehouse, followed by the unmistakable sound of men's voices shouting orders. Viktor's men were here. They had arrived.

Alex's hand instinctively shot out, grabbing Zara's arm, pulling her toward a hidden alcove where shadows could shield them. They crouched low, their hearts pounding in their chests, the adrenaline making everything seem sharper, more vivid.

"They've found us," Alex whispered, his voice low but steady. "They're coming."

Zara felt her stomach drop as the sound of boots echoed closer. She wanted to run. She wanted to get out of there and never look back. But she couldn't. Not anymore. Not with everything they had sacrificed, not with everything they had fought for. She couldn't afford to back down now.

She gripped her weapon tighter, her fingers slipping slightly on the cold metal. She had been in dangerous situations before, but this was different. This wasn't just about survival. This was personal. Viktor had made it personal the moment he'd set his sights on Alex. And now, Alex was taking a stand—whether Zara was ready for it or not.

"They're close," Alex muttered, his voice tense. "Stay low. Stay quiet."

Zara nodded, her breath shallow, her eyes trained on the shadows ahead. The warehouse was dark, but she could make out the faint movement of figures through the haze. Viktor's men were closing in. They were searching for them, determined to wipe out the threat once and for all.

The Final Test

Then, the first figure appeared—a tall man, his face hidden in the shadows. He moved cautiously, scanning the area, his eyes flicking over every corner, every potential hiding place. Alex held his breath, his body tensed, ready to spring into action at the slightest movement.

Zara's heart raced as the man came closer, his footsteps slow and deliberate. He passed right in front of them, inches from where Zara was hiding, and for a moment, it felt as though time had stopped. She could hear the man's breathing, could see the gun holstered at his side. She felt the weight of the situation like a physical presence, pressing down on her chest, making every muscle in her body scream to run, to hide.

But she stayed still, her body pressed tightly against the cold wall, every muscle locked in place. She knew that if they were discovered now, they wouldn't survive. Viktor's men were too powerful, too well-trained. It wasn't just about outsmarting them anymore—it was about surviving long enough to strike first.

The man moved past them, and Zara's breath left her in a relieved rush. But there was no time to celebrate. The sound of more footsteps echoed, and Zara knew that they didn't have much longer before their position would be compromised.

"On my mark," Alex whispered, his voice tight with focus. "We move. We make it to the storage room. Then we wait for the signal."

Zara nodded, her stomach twisted into knots. It was the only plan they had, the only option left. She had to trust him. She had to trust that this was the right move. She was scared, so scared, but she knew that they were too far in to back down now.

Alex moved silently, his movements fluid, instinctive. Zara followed, staying as close as she could, her heart in her throat as they made their way toward the storage room. Every step felt like an eternity, the seconds dragging out as the sounds of Viktor's men grew louder, closer.

Then, just as they reached the entrance to the storage room, a loud shout rang out from behind them.

"Stop right there!"

Zara froze. Her heart slammed against her ribs as she turned to see a man standing in the doorway, his gun raised, eyes locked on them. The tension in the air thickened as the standoff began.

Alex's eyes narrowed, his posture tense as he took a step forward, his gun pointed at the man. "This ends now."

The man smirked, his hand gripping the gun tighter as he stepped closer. "You think you can stop us? You think you can outsmart Viktor?"

Alex's voice was cold, his words laced with anger. "I don't need to outsmart Viktor. I just need to end this."

And just like that, the fight began.

The Final Test

In a flash, Alex lunged forward, firing his weapon with precision. The man crumpled to the ground, his body falling with a sickening thud. Alex didn't hesitate. He turned to Zara, his face a mask of determination, but there was something else there too—something raw, something desperate.

"Now, Zara," he said, his voice hard with urgency. "We run."

Zara's body moved on instinct, her feet pounding against the concrete as they sprinted toward the back of the warehouse, the sounds of gunfire and chaos echoing behind them. The world had turned into a blur, a haze of adrenaline and fear. But even in the midst of the chaos, one thought burned through her mind: this was it. This was the final test.

And they were going to fight until the end.

The world around them had unraveled, and now, there was no going back.

Fifteen

The Truth

The sounds of the gunfire were distant now, muffled by the cold concrete walls and the panic that gripped Zara's chest. She had followed Alex through the shadows of the warehouse, adrenaline surging through her veins, but now, standing at the heart of the chaos, she was beginning to feel the weight of everything—the weight of the lies, the secrets, and the betrayal that had spiraled around her like a storm she couldn't escape. It was all too much.

Alex had said they were going to fight until the end, but Zara wasn't sure anymore if she had the strength to keep up with him. She had never asked for this life, never signed up for the war between Viktor and Alex, between his father's empire and the rival who wanted to destroy it. But here she was, in the middle of it all, surrounded by blood and violence, unsure of who she could trust or how much longer she could survive.

The Truth

She glanced over at Alex, his face a mask of determination. He was focused, his eyes scanning the room for any threat, any movement that could signal danger. He had always been the one to keep them alive, to guide them through the darkness. But tonight, Zara wasn't so sure if even Alex could keep them from falling.

"Zara," Alex's voice cut through the silence, sharp and urgent. "Stay close."

Zara nodded, her heart hammering in her chest. She had no choice but to follow him. He had been her rock, her anchor, in a world that was constantly shifting beneath her feet. But in the back of her mind, she couldn't shake the thought that something wasn't right—that even Alex was hiding something from her. There was a depth to him she couldn't understand, a side to his life that had remained locked away, even from her.

The two of them moved through the abandoned building, their footsteps echoing in the empty space. The shadows seemed to stretch and twist around them, making every corner feel like an unknown danger. But despite the fear that gnawed at Zara's insides, she couldn't help but be drawn to Alex. There was something about him, something in the way he carried himself, that kept her from walking away. No matter how much the world around them threatened to collapse, she knew deep down that she couldn't leave him. Not again.

"Where are we going?" Zara asked, her voice barely above a whisper, her words lost in the quiet tension that hung in the air. "What's the plan now?"

Alex didn't answer at first. He kept moving, his gaze flicking over the darkened corners of the room. When he finally spoke, his voice was low, almost pained. "We need to get to the safehouse. It's the only place we'll be able to regroup."

Zara frowned, her brow furrowing with confusion. "Safehouse? I thought you said we were done running, Alex. I thought we were going to face Viktor together, not hide away."

Alex's eyes darkened as he turned toward her, his face hardening with a mixture of frustration and regret. "I'm not hiding, Zara. But there are things you don't understand—things I need to explain to you before it's too late."

Zara's heart skipped a beat. "Explain? Alex, I'm so tired of not knowing the truth. Every time I think I've got a handle on this, you throw me into another lie. I don't even know who you are anymore."

The words hung in the air between them, thick with accusation and fear. For the first time, Alex didn't look like the man she had come to love. For the first time, he looked like someone she didn't recognize—a stranger whose motives had always been hidden behind layers of secrets.

"I'm sorry," Alex said, his voice hoarse, his eyes filled with pain. "I didn't want to lie to you. I never meant to drag you into this world, but it's too late. You're already in it. And now, I have to protect you. I have to protect us."

Zara shook her head, her frustration rising. "But you didn't

The Truth

protect me. You used me. You used me to hide from your father, from Viktor. I was never part of your plan, Alex. You just kept me in the dark until it was too late."

"I never meant to use you," Alex whispered, his voice strained with emotion. "I thought I was protecting you by keeping you away from the truth. I thought I could shield you from this world, but now, it's all coming to a head. And I can't protect you anymore, Zara. Not without you knowing everything."

Zara's breath hitched as his words finally sunk in. "What do you mean?" she asked, her voice trembling. "What is it you haven't told me? What's the truth?"

Alex paused, his shoulders sagging as if the weight of everything finally became too much for him to carry alone. "The truth is that I've never been free. Not really. Not the way you think."

Zara's heart pounded in her chest, the words ringing in her ears. "What do you mean? What are you talking about?"

He turned away from her, his back stiff as he walked toward the far wall, his hand pressed to his forehead as if gathering the strength to speak. "I'm not just running from Viktor, Zara. I've been running from my own family. From my father's legacy. And now, it's all coming back to me. Viktor doesn't just want me, he wants the empire. He wants to destroy everything my father built, and to do that, he needs to break me. But the truth is, I'm not just trying to escape him. I'm trying to escape myself."

Zara's mind raced, her thoughts colliding with each other,

trying to make sense of what he had just said. She stepped closer, her voice shaking with confusion and hurt. "What does that even mean, Alex? You're not just trying to escape Viktor… you're trying to escape yourself? How can you expect me to understand that? How can I understand you if you don't even understand yourself?"

Alex turned to face her, his eyes filled with raw emotion. "Because I'm the son of a monster, Zara. I've been groomed for this my whole life. Every decision, every step I've taken, has been controlled. My father, Viktor, they're two sides of the same coin. And I've spent my whole life running from them, from the things they want me to be. But the truth is, Zara… I'm not just running from them. I'm running from everything they've made me into."

Zara's breath caught in her throat as she tried to process his words. She had known Alex had been hiding something, but this? This was a truth she hadn't been prepared for. She had always known there was darkness in his past, in his family, but she never imagined it was this deep. She had trusted him, had let him in, and now she was faced with the reality that everything she had believed was based on a lie.

"Then what do we do now, Alex?" Zara asked, her voice barely above a whisper. "What is this all for? If we're just running from your past, from your family, how can we ever truly be free?"

Alex's expression softened, his eyes filled with a mixture of sorrow and resolve. He stepped closer to her, his voice low and raw. "We fight. We fight for what we want. We fight for a future where we don't have to live in the shadow of my father's legacy, where we can choose who we want to be. This fight isn't just about me anymore, Zara. It's about us. It's about finding freedom in the truth, even if that truth is ugly."

Zara felt a flicker of hope, a fragile spark of something she hadn't felt in a long time. The truth—no matter how painful—was the only thing that could set them free. And in that moment, she realized that she had to make a choice. She had to choose whether to stay and fight with Alex, or to walk away from everything they had built together.

Her heart beat in her chest, steady now, as she made her decision. She reached out to him, her fingers brushing against his, the touch sending a shock of warmth through her.

"I'm with you," she said, her voice strong, her heart clear. "No matter what happens. I'm with you."

Alex's eyes softened, a mixture of relief and something deeper flashing across his face. "We'll get through this. Together. I promise."

And in that moment, as they stood together in the heart of the storm, the truth that had been buried for so long finally began to set them free. They weren't running anymore. They weren't hiding. They were ready to face the future, whatever it might bring. Together.

www.ingramcontent.com/pod-product-compliance
Lightning Source LLC
LaVergne TN
LVHW020423080526
838202LV00055B/5022